D0934009

*B*e who you are.
There's only one you,
and you are great!

Other Titles in This Series:

223 Great Things About Mothers

223 Great Things About Sisters

223 Great Things to Always Remember

We wish to thank Rachel Snyder, Lisa Truesdale, and the Blue Mountain Arts creative staff for contributing writings to this collection.

We gratefully acknowledge permission granted by Susan Polis Schutz to reprint "There are many people...." Copyright © 1983 by Stephen Schutz and Susan Polis Schutz. And Rachel Snyder for "Remember what you're made of." Copyright © 2008 by Rachel Snyder. And Walker Publishing Company, Inc., for "Having fun doesn't..." from GIRL TALK by Judith Harlan. Copyright © 1997 by Judith Harlan. Reprinted by permission. All rights reserved.

Library of Congress Control Number: 2008908553
ISBN: 978-1-59842-366-2

Blue Mountain Arts, Inc.
P.O. Box 4549, Boulder, Colorado 80306

223

Great Things

TEENS

Should Do

Blue Mountain Press™
Boulder, Colorado

Great Things Every
TEEN
Should Do...

- Believe in yourself. A little self-confidence goes a long way.

- Speak your mind.

- Love yourself no matter what.

- Remember: you really can do anything you set your mind to.

6 Stretch yourself! Try at least one new thing every week.

6 Attend a poetry reading or an art gallery opening.

6 Learn a magic trick.

6 Open the dictionary to a random page and learn the definition of the first word you see. If you already know that word, try again.

⚅ Next time you go to your favorite restaurant, choose something from the menu you've never ordered before.

⚅ Memorize some interesting bits of trivia. You never know when they might come in handy.

⚅ Enter a poem, picture, song, recipe, story, or great idea in a contest. You just might win!

⚅ Start a blog or create your own website.

G Be an individual. It's easy
to follow the crowd, but it's
so much more interesting and
fulfilling to follow your heart.

G Know what matters most
to you. Make a list to help
you remember.

G Be outrageous when
everybody's looking.

G Act silly sometimes.

Do a cartwheel if you feel like it.

G Let yourself be touched by a sad movie or a book with an unhappy ending. Go ahead and cry.

G Cut yourself some slack: nobody's perfect! Everything is turning upside down around you and inside you, so you're bound to feel mixed up and confused sometimes.

G Walk in someone else's shoes for a day — not literally, but try to imagine how it would feel to be someone besides yourself.

ᴳ Remember the Golden Rule: treat others the way you want them to treat you.

ᴳ Smile or say hi to someone you don't know. You might just make that person's day.

ᴳ Find a mentor — someone older whose personality and lifestyle you admire.

ᴳ Be a mentor to someone younger than yourself.

Decisions are incredibly important things!
Good decisions will come back to bless you.
Bad decisions can come back to haunt you.

That's why it's so important that you take
the time to choose wisely.

Choose to do the things that will reflect
well... on your ability, your integrity,
your spirit, your health, your tomorrows,
your smiles, your dreams, and yourself.

— Douglas Pagels

⑥ Respect the opinions and
choices of others — but always
make up your own mind.

⑥ Listen to your gut feelings.
If something doesn't feel quite
right, it probably isn't.

⑥ Make a list of your very best
qualities and hang it on your
mirror to look at when you
get ready each morning.

⑥ Use your mind *and* your
heart to make decisions.

☛ Keep a journal where you can write down your feelings and dreams.

☛ Never compromise or change yourself just to get someone to like you.

☛ Take responsibility.

☛ Give yourself a hug every once in a while.

☞ Be confident.

☞ Be authentic.

☞ Be inquisitive.

☞ Be spontaneous.

☞ Be sensitive.

☞ Be enthusiastic.

☞ Be adventurous.

☞ Be compassionate.

ᴳ Let your voice be heard. Send letters to newspapers, websites, magazines, and your congressperson.

ᴳ Make a handmade birthday card for someone you care about.

ᴳ Create a special place in your room for displaying photos of people you admire, inspirational words you've read or written, and objects that have special meaning to you.

ᴳ Take a picture of yourself or draw a self-portrait. You might not realize it now, but you look amazing.

☞ Let your creativity flow...

Paint, dance, sing, draw, write, or sculpt.

ᘓ Set a goal and stick with it, even if it's something as simple as getting up ten minutes earlier or growing out your bangs.

ᘓ Make sure your schedule includes time to do nothing in particular.

ᘓ Host a dinner party for your friends.

ᘓ Reduce the drama in your life. It's not worth the time and energy.

G Explore your interests no matter how unusual they might be.

G Choose clothes that reflect your own personal style.

G Create a holiday tradition.

G Rearrange your room. Changing your surroundings can change the way you think about your world.

Having fun doesn't have to end with childhood. Having fun is simply holding on to the joy of each day. It's looking up at the sky and taking a deep breath just because it feels good. It's laughing at the shapes in clouds and dancing in the rain. It's letting go of the "should" voices that tell you that you should settle down.

— Judith Harlan

๏ Play on a playground.

๏ Laugh loud, often,
and from the heart.

๏ Color with crayons. It's not
just for preschoolers!

๏ Ride your bike.

๏ Keep believing in magic, in
angels, and in miracles —
no matter how old you are.

⚅ Wake up early enough to see the sunrise at least once a year.

⚅ Listen to the natural sounds around you: the song of a bird, the wind in the trees, the crack of thunder.

⚅ Walk in the rain without an umbrella.

⚅ Stroll barefoot on the beach and wiggle your toes in the sand.

⚅ Lie in the grass when it's nice outside.

G Unplug yourself from your electronic world (computers, phones, video games, and digital music players) for at least an hour a day.

G Make a collage with pictures you cut out of magazines that depict things you like to do or ideals you believe in.

G Build something. It could be a birdhouse, a shelf, or a picture frame.

Take control of your own education...

The more you learn now,
the better off you'll be later.

ᕬ Before you start your homework,
take five minutes to empty your
mind of unnecessary thoughts.

ᕬ When you think you've studied
enough for a test, study just a
little bit more.

ᕬ Don't just cram to get through the
next exam and then forget everything
you learned. Your world will be so
much richer if you retain the information.

ᕬ Allow yourself to ask for help.

Get organized...

G Take a few minutes every evening to prepare for the next day. Choose your outfit; pack your lunch; put your homework in your backpack.

G Keep all your important papers together in one place.

G Clean out your closet.

G Store away things from your childhood you want to keep but no longer use.

G On Monday make a list of everything
   you need to do by Friday. On Friday
   if everything is checked off on your
   list, treat yourself to something special.

G ~~Have one small notebook for recording
   phone numbers and addresses.~~

G If you've taken on too much to do,
   learn to prioritize, and then next time
   learn to say no.

G Don't let fear of failure ever hold you back... just go for it!

G Audition for a play.

G Start a band.

G Memorize a poem.

G Join the Sp~~an~~ish club, debate club, or ch~~ess~~ club.

Any club

Try out for the team.

6 Try a new hairstyle.

6 Go to a church or synagogue you haven't been to before — just to see what it's like.

6 Apply for an internship in a field that interests you.

6 Add color to your life! Paint your room; hang a prism in your window; wear brightly colored shirts or shoes.

G Surprise someone who underestimated you. It's a great feeling.

G Write a real letter to someone you miss. Put something special in the envelope, like a photograph or a pressed flower.

G Read a classic novel.

G On your next birthday, collect gifts to give to teens who need them more than you do.

There are many people
that we meet in our lives
but only a very few
will make a lasting impression
on our minds and hearts
These people will always
listen and talk to you
They will care about
your happiness and well-being
They will like you for who you are
and they will support you at all times
It is these rare people that we will
think of often
and who will always remain
important to us
as true friends

— *Susan Polis Schutz*

ତ Choose friends who do not judge
other people, and work hard not
to make judgments yourself.

ତ Invite that new kid to hang
out one day after school.

ତ Hold on to your old friends. Even
if you find you're growing apart,
remember that they're the ones
who know and understand you best.

ତ Seek out friends of all ages.
You'll be amazed how fun
they can be.

If you're feeling stressed-out...

🙢 Close your eyes and take a
few slow, deep breaths.

🙢 Squeeze a stress ball.

🙢 Make really funny faces at
yourself in the mirror.

🙢 Think about one of your
happiest memories.

🙢 Take a walk to clear your mind.

🙢 Turn on some relaxing music.

ᕮ When you're faced with big problems, break them down into tiny steps. Then take one small step at a time.

ᕮ Make up a positive affirmation like "I love myself" or "I can do anything." Repeat it to yourself whenever you're feeling scared or insecure.

ᕮ Remember: things often aren't as bad as they seem.

Be informed about what's
going on in the world...

Read the newspaper, check the
headlines online, or watch the news.

ᴳ Get political. Support a cause
that resonates with you.

ᴳ Register to vote when
you're old enough.

ᴳ Volunteer for an organization
you care about, like an animal
shelter, food bank, or senior center.

ᴳ Every issue has at least two
points of view: be willing to
consider them all before you
make up your mind.

G Try your best not to take everything
personally. It's not always about
you, even if it feels and sounds and
looks that way.

G Remember that you can't control what
other people think or how they act.
You can only control your own
thoughts and actions.

G If something is bothering you, don't
keep it bottled up inside. Talk about it
to a friend, a relative, or even to
yourself. Just giving voice to a problem
will make you feel a lot better.

๒ If you've done something that hurt someone, admit to what you've done and offer a sincere apology.

๒ There will always be words you should have said and things you should or shouldn't have done. Don't allow yourself to get hung up on regrets.

๒ Focus on today. You can't get back yesterday and you don't know what will happen tomorrow.

G Sing in the shower at the top of your lungs — even if you can't carry a tune.

G Listen to an audio book.

G Learn to play a musical instrument — even if it's just a kazoo.

G When you're home alone, turn up the stereo and dance.

ⓖ Explore your musical tastes...

Try listening to bands
you've never heard before.

G Get comfortable being with yourself. You're always available for a walk, a movie, a bike ride, or a swim, even if no one else is.

G Don't let other people tell you who you are.

G Celebrate your uniqueness.

G Accept that not everybody will like you (and that's okay). Just make sure that you like yourself.

Learn to forgive...

⑥ Forgive yourself for messing up.

⑥ Forgive your friends for saying unkind words.

⑥ Forgive your parents for embarrassing you in public. (They can't help it!)

⑥ Forgive you-know-who for doing you-know-what.

Being a teenager can be difficult at times, but through it all, you will learn about who you are, who you want to be, and what it will take for you to become that person. In the end, it will all be worth it.

— *Amy Michele Shockey*

ᴳ Make an effort to smile when you are unhappy. Soon your mind will follow your lips' lead and you'll be smiling on the inside, too.

ᴳ Accept that you'll make mistakes in life — lots of them! Just do the best you can and try not to make the same mistake twice.

ᴳ When you're going through tough times, remember that they will not last forever.

G Have the courage to talk to people face to face. Accept that sometimes e-mail and texting just will not do.

G Trust your intuition.

G Express yourself: say what you mean and learn how to speak and write with style and authority.

G Learn the basic rules of grammar and punctuation.

6 Pay attention to how people are the same instead of how they're different.

6 Speak up for those who aren't able to speak up for themselves.

6 Be a leader instead of a follower.

6 When things get too hot to handle, walk away — or run if you must.

ᘖ Pick up a piece of trash even if
you aren't the one who dropped it.

ᘖ Reuse that bag, that box,
that paper.

ᘖ Eat locally grown fruits and veggies.

ᘖ Turn off the lights when you
leave a room. You'll be saving
money and the environment.

Plant a garden and watch it grow.

ᵷ Be grateful for what you have.

ᵷ Choose your battles and always try to be the bigger person. Just because another person is rude or insulting doesn't mean you have to be rude or insulting back.

ᵷ Do something nice for someone else every day, like holding a door open, offering half of your candy bar, or letting someone go ahead of you in line.

ᵷ Do something nice for yourself every day, too.

G Call your mother for no reason
at all.

G Interview your grandparents. Ask
about their accomplishments in life.
Find out how, when, and where
they met.

G Listen to your parents' advice. Most
of the time, they really do know
what they're talking about — they
were teenagers once, too.

G Be proud of your heritage and
don't be afraid to show it!

Remember what you're made of. Remember what's flowing in your veins. Remember what you were given, and remember what you went out and created on your own. Like any great masterpiece, you're not done yet. Inside you is the best of everyone who has come before you — and the best of everyone yet to be. You can forget some of what life hands you, but never ever forget who you are.

— Rachel Snyder

ଓ Look at yourself in the mirror and
be happy with what you see.

ଓ Choose boyfriends or girlfriends
who treat you with respect.

ଓ Keep in mind that crushes almost
always fade, but friendships can
last a lifetime.

ଓ Tell someone you love how
much they mean to you.

ᴳ If you're feeling insecure about something, choose not to let it bother you. Do this often enough, and eventually you'll develop confidence you never knew you had.

ᴳ When someone pays you a compliment, don't shrug it off. Accept it graciously and say thank you.

ᴳ Wear your bike helmet. Messing up your hair is way better than messing up your head!

ᴳ Start a fashion trend.

G Don't be afraid to laugh at yourself.

G Always be honest. It may sound cliché, but truthfulness is a measure of a person's character.

G Try for an entire day not to judge or criticize anybody or anything.

G Bake cookies to give to your friends.

G Run for student-body president.

Open a savings account.

ⓖ Before you spend a lot of money on the latest "cool" thing, make sure it's something you really want (not just something everyone else has).

ⓖ Learn to calculate in your head the total cost of your purchase before going to the register.

ⓖ Donate some of your savings to charity every year.

ⓖ Learn how to read a bank statement and balance a checking account.

G If something unfamiliar, painful, or mysterious is going on in your body, find a health-care professional who's easy to talk to.

G Try to get some exercise every day.

G Eat a banana or apple with your lunch instead of a plate of greasy French fries.

G Give your teeth lots of tender, loving care. You only get one set, and it's hard to chew, talk, and smile without them.

ɢ Kick your bad habits. If you're doing something that makes you sick or makes you feel bad about yourself, stop doing it. Ask for help if you need to.

ɢ Wear sunscreen (even on cloudy days).

ɢ Drink lots of water.

ɢ Never underestimate the power of lots of sleep! Your body, your mind, and your spirit all need it.

ᴳ Do things that make you uncomfortable, like taking a ballroom dancing class or reading a book about astrophysics. You might find a new passion.

ᴳ Invent something.

ᴳ Awesome stuff happens everywhere — not just on TV. Check out your favorite shows, but remember that there is a wide, unpredictable world to explore.

ᴳ Thank a teacher.

⌐ Be curious about everything...

Ask lots of questions and
find lots of answers.

Learn how to...

- Speak a second language.

- Parallel park.

- Eat with chopsticks.

- Check the oil in your car.

- Tie a necktie.

- Sew on a button.

ᴕ Read a map.

ᴕ Perform CPR.

ᴕ Drive a stick shift.

ᴕ Speak comfortably in public.

ᴕ Change a flat tire.

ᴕ Cook your favorite meal.

*You may not understand
just how much your life means
to those around you —
how people's days are brighter
    because you're here
and the sound of your laughter
touches the hearts of everyone
    around you.*

*Your presence adds something special
    and invaluable to the world.
Though you may not realize it,
    your life is a gift that is treasured.*

— Star Nakamoto

ᴳ Embrace what makes you different.
It might be your curly hair, your
math skills, your freckles, or your
piano-playing talent.

ᴳ Everybody has strengths and
weaknesses. Get to know
what yours are.

ᴳ Think about the people you most
admire and why. Then try to
incorporate the things you like
about them into your own life.

- Start collecting something. It could be stamps, coins, first-edition books, or anything you find interesting.

- Get a summer job.

- Try a new sport, like snowboarding, badminton, or karate.

- Climb a mountain.

ᴳ Think before you do something you can't undo. This includes saying something mean or getting a tattoo.

ᴳ Don't place too much importance on your looks. There's so much more to you than your appearance.

ᴳ Resist the urge to compare yourself to anyone else. You are the only "you" there will ever be.

⊙ Every so often, look at a map
of the world and ask yourself
where you would like to go.
How can you make that
adventure a reality?

⊙ Don't give up. Practice really
does make perfect, so just
keep at it.

⊙ Borrow a telescope and stargaze.

⊙ Don't accept the world the way
it is — question it, challenge it,
change it... make it better.

Dream big, bigger...

Dream the biggest dream you can.

G Save things — your diaries, artwork, letters, and photographs. You'll enjoy looking back on them someday.

G Know that no matter how awkward, scared, self-conscious, hopeless, confused, or crazy you're feeling, other teens are feeling the exact same way. You're not alone.

G Think about your future, but don't think too hard. You've got plenty of time.

Savor your teen years by taking time to...

⚸ Have fun.

⚸ Learn.

⚸ Grow.

⚸ Feel.

⚸ Discover.

⚸ Achieve.

⚸ Experience.

⚸ Enjoy every minute.

And most of all, always remember to...

be you!